Pebble

Great African-Americans

Thurgood
MARSHALL

by Luke Colins   Consulting Editor: Gail Saunders-Smith, PhD

CAPSTONE PRESS
a capstone imprint

Pebble Books are published by Capstone Press,
1710 Roe Crest Drive, North Mankato, Minnesota 56003
www.capstonepub.com

Library of Congress Cataloging-in-Publication Data
Colins, Luke.
Thurgood Marshall / by Luke Colins.
pages cm. — (Pebble Books. Great African-Americans)
Includes bibliographical references and index.
Summary: "Simple text and photographs present the life of Thurgood Marshall"– Provided by
publisher.
  ISBN 978-1-4765-3956-0 (library binding)
  ISBN 978-1-4765-5160-9 (paperback)
  ISBN 978-1-4765-6017-5 (ebook)
1. Marshall, Thurgood, 1908-1993—Juvenile literature. 2. United States. Supreme
Court—Officials and employees—Biography—Juvenile literature. 3. African American judges—
Biography—Juvenile literature. I. Title.
  KF8745.M34C65 2014
  347.73'2634–dc23
  [B]   2013037676

Editorial Credits
Anna Butzer, editor; Ashlee Suker, designer; Wanda Winch, media researcher;
Laura Manthe, production specialist

Photo Credits
AP Images, 16, 20, Courtesy of the NAACP, 14; Coris: Bettmann, cover, 4, 12, 18; Library of
Congress: Prints and Photographs Division, 6; Newscom: Picture History, 10; Shutterstock:
justasc, (gavel design); Scurlock Studio Records/Archives Center, National Musuem of
American History, Behring Center, Smithsonian Institution, 8

Note to Parents and Teachers

The Great African-Americans set supports national curriculum standards for
social studies related to people, places, and environments. This book describes and
illustrates Thurgood Marshall. The images support early readers in understanding
the text. The repetition of words and phrases helps early readers learn new words.
This book also introduces early readers to subject-specific vocabulary words, which
are defined in the Glossary section. Early readers may need assistance to read
some words and to use the Table of Contents, Glossary, Read More, Internet Sites,
and Index sections of the book.

Printed in the United States of America in North Mankato, Minnesota.
092013   007764CGS14

Table of Contents

4

Meet Thurgood

Thurgood Marshall was the first
African-American justice on
the U.S. Supreme Court.
He was also a lawyer. He fought
for equal rights for all people.

a group of African-
American students in
Maryland in the 1930s

1908

born in Maryland

Young Thurgood

Thurgood was born July 2, 1908, in Maryland. Segregation was legal when Thurgood was growing up. He went to a school for only black children. Thurgood saw that African-Americans were not treated the same as whites.

1908

born in Maryland

Thurgood graduated from Lincoln University in 1930. He applied to law school at the University of Maryland. Thurgood was turned down because he was not white. He attended Howard University instead. Both blacks and whites went to Howard.

Thurgood (left) and client Donald Murray

1908

born in Maryland

1933

graduates from
Howard Law School;
starts own law practice

Thurgood graduated first
in his class in 1933. He started
his own law practice in Baltimore.
In 1935 he won an important
court case. He sued the University
of Maryland for not allowing an
African-American student to attend.

Thurgood (center) in Washington, D.C.

1908
born in Maryland

1933
graduates from
Howard Law School;
starts own law practice

1934
begins working
for the NAACP

12

As an Adult

Thurgood worked on equal rights cases. In 1934 Thurgood began working for the National Association for the Advancement of Colored People (NAACP). He wanted to help defend the rights of African-Americans.

Thurgood (second from right) and other lawyers for the NAACP

1908

1933

1934

born in Maryland

graduates from
Howard Law School;
starts own law practice

begins working
for the NAACP

In 1938 Thurgood became
a full-time lawyer for the NAACP.
Some of his cases went to the
U.S. Supreme Court. Thurgood won
29 of 32 cases that went through
the Supreme Court.

Thurgood (center) after he won Brown vs. Board of Education

1908

born in Maryland

1933

graduates from Howard Law School; starts own law practice

1934

begins working for the NAACP

Later Years

Thurgood was awarded the Spingarn Medal in 1946. This award is given each year to an outstanding African-American. In 1954 he won the case *Brown v. Board of Education.* This decision made school segregation illegal.

1954

wins *Brown v. Board of Education*

Thurgood (top right) and the other eight Supreme Court justices in 1967

1908

born in Maryland

1933

graduates from Howard Law School; starts own law practice

1934

begins working for the NAACP

In 1967 President Lyndon Johnson named Thurgood to the Supreme Court. Thurgood became the first African-American Supreme Court justice. Thurgood fought for the rights of American Indians, women, and the poor.

1954

wins *Brown v. Board of Education*

1967

named justice on the U.S. Supreme Court

Thurgood with his wife and children in 1961

1908

born in Maryland

1933

graduates from Howard Law School; starts own law practice

1934

begins working for the NAACP

Thurgood was a U.S. Supreme Court justice for 24 years. His decisions helped protect the rights of everyone. Thurgood retired in 1991. He died in 1993 at the age of 84. People remember him as a great lawyer and a great justice.

1954
wins *Brown v. Board of Education*

1967
named justice on the U.S. Supreme Court

1991
retires from the Supreme Court

1993
dies at the age of 84

Glossary

defend—to try to keep something from being changed or harmed

equal rights—the ability for everyone to be able to have the same just, moral, or rightful things

illegal—against the law

justice—a member of the U.S. Supreme Court

lawyer—a person who is trained to advise people about the law

retire—to give up work usually because of a person's age

segregation—separating people because of their skin color

U.S. Supreme Court—the highest court in the United States

Read More

Jeffrey, Gary. *Thurgood Marshall: The Supreme Court Rules on "Separate but Equal."* New York: Gareth Stevens Pub., 2013.

Linde, Barbara M. *Thurgood Marshall.* Civil Rights Crusaders. New York: Gareth Stevens Pub., 2012.

Schuh, Mari. *The U.S. Supreme Court.* The U.S. Government. North Mankato, Minn.: Capstone Press, 2012.

Internet Sites

FactHound offers a safe, fun way to find Internet sites related to this book. All of the sites on FactHound have been researched by our staff.

Here's all you do:
Visit *www.facthound.com*
Type in this code: 9781476539560

Super-cool stuff!   Check out projects, games and lots more at
www.capstonekids.com

Critical Thinking Using the Common Core

1. Keeping people apart because of their skin color is called segregation. Why do you think Thurgood worked so hard to end segregation? (Integration of Knowledge and Ideas)

2. Thurgood felt that it was important for everyone to have equal rights. What did he do to help people who were not treated equally? (Integration of Knowledge and Ideas)

Index

Word Count: 220
Grade: 1
Early-Intervention Level: 22